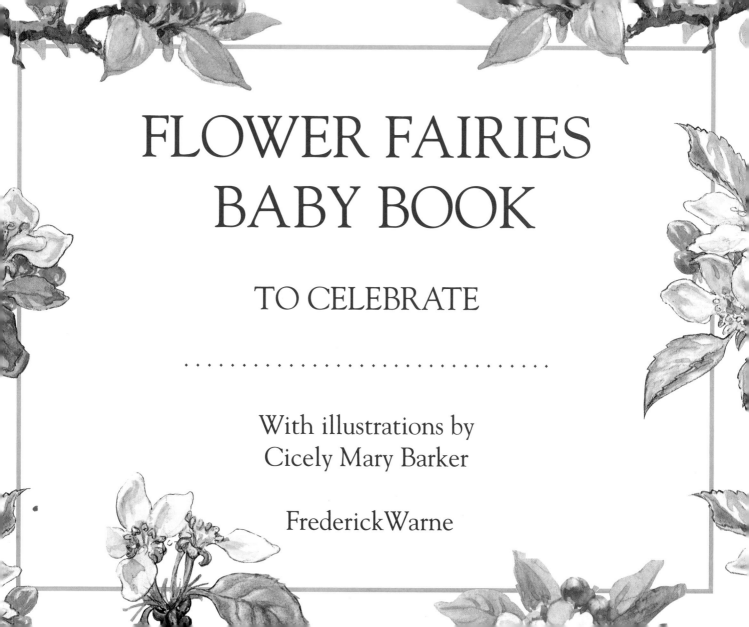

FLOWER FAIRIES
BABY BOOK

TO CELEBRATE

. . . .

With illustrations by
Cicely Mary Barker

Frederick Warne

BIRTH FLOWERS

January	Snowdrop	Hope
February	Primrose	Loyalty
March	Daffodil	Compassion
April	Daisies	Innocence
May	Lily-of-the-Valley	Elegance
June	Rose	Love
July	Water Lily	Purity of heart
August	Lavender	Trust
September	Aster	Generosity
October	Heliotrope	Devotion
November	Chrysanthemum	Truth
December	Holly	Foresight

BIRTH

I was born on . . . .

at . . . . (time)

Day of the week . . . .

Place . . . .

. . . .

Doctor . . . .

BIRTH

When I was born

I weighed . . . .

I measured . . . .

My eyes were . . . .

My hair was . . . .

My parents thought I looked like . . . .

. . . .

. . . .

(photo)

Aged . . . .

BIRTH

My first visitors were . . . .

. . . .

My birth was announced like this . . . .

(stick down card or
newspaper cutting)

BIRTH

On the day I was born

The news headlines were . . . .

. . . .

. . . .

The weather was . . . .

The number 1 record was . . . .

. . . .

FAMILY TREE

Grandfather   Grandmother   Grandfather   Grandmother

. . . .

. . . .

Father   Mother

. . . .

Brothers   Sisters

. . . .

. . . .

Baby

. . . .

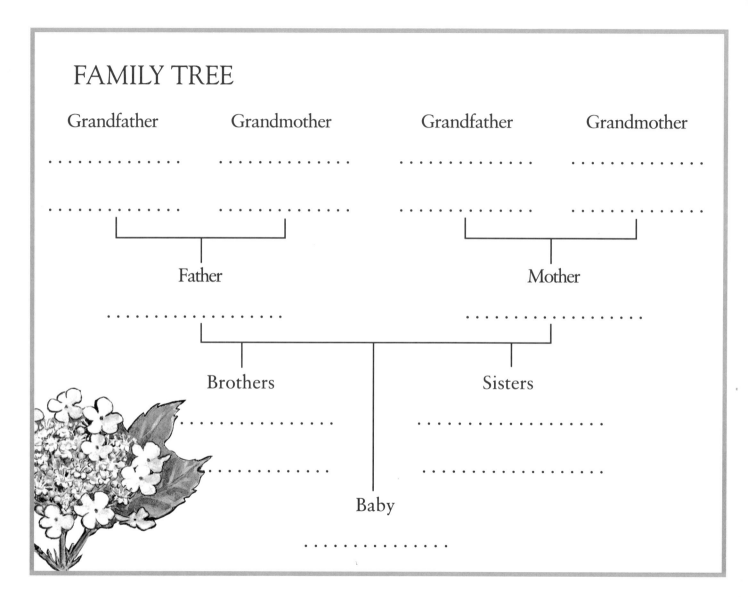

FAMILY

I have . . . . brothers and

. . . . sisters

We live at . . . .

. . . .

. . . .

Our pets are . . . .

. . . .

NAMES

My full names are . . . .

. . . .

. . . .

They were chosen because . . . .

. . . .

. . . .

. . . .

NAMES

I was given my names on

Date . . . .

Place . . . .

The guests were . . . .

. . . .

. . . .

. . . .   Aged . . . .

My presents were . . . .

(photo)

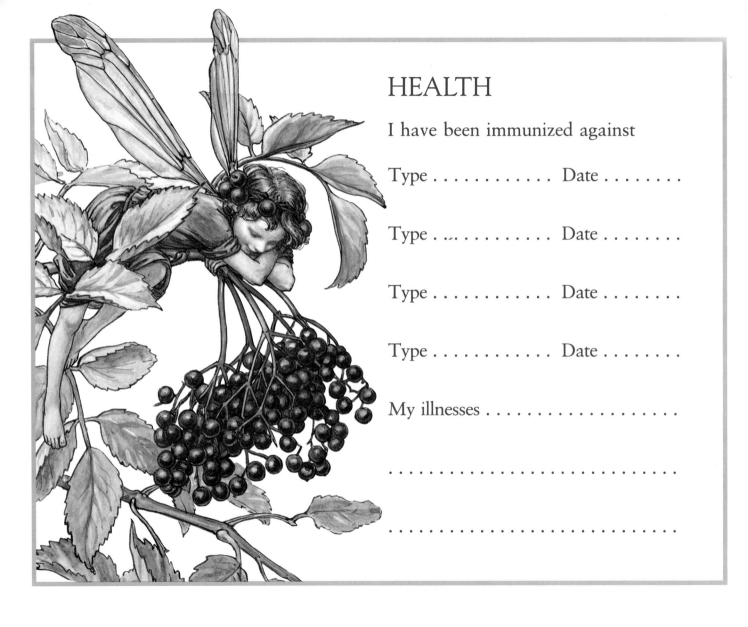

HEALTH

I have been immunized against

Type . . . . Date . . . .

Type . . . . Date . . . .

Type . . . . Date . . . .

Type . . . . Date . . . .

My illnesses . . . .

. . . .

. . . .

HEALTH

Various flowers, plants, herbs and spices are believed by many to have medicinal powers. Some of these natural remedies are, perhaps, just old wives' tales but undoubtedly flowers and plants can be used to cure some aches and pains. A simple example is rubbing dock leaves or mint leaves on a rash caused by stinging nettles to soothe the irritation. Insect bites can also be made less painful by rubbing gently with marigold leaves. A toothache can be dulled by applying oil of cloves.

I cut my teeth on

1 . . . .

2 . . . .

3 . . . .

4 . . . .

5 . . . .

Upper

Right   Left

Lower

Number the chart

6 . . . .

7 . . . .

8 . . . .

9 . . . .

10 . . . .

DEVELOPMENT

HEIGHT AND WEIGHT CHART

Months	Weight	Height
1	. . . .	. . . .
2	. . . .	. . . .
3	. . . .	. . . .
4	. . . .	. . . .
5	. . . .	. . . .
6	. . . .	. . . .
7	. . . .	. . . .
8	. . . .	. . . .
9	. . . .	. . . .
10	. . . .	. . . .
11	. . . .	. . . .
12	. . . .	. . . .

DEVELOPMENT

My handprint   My footprint

THE SONG OF
THE APPLE BLOSSOM FAIRIES

Up in the tree we see you, blossom-babies,
　　All pink and white;
We think there must be fairies to protect you
　　From frost and blight,
Until, some windy day, in drifts of petals,
　　You take your flight.

You'll fly away! But if we wait with patience,
　　Some day we'll find
Here, in your place, full-grown and ripe, the apples
　　You left behind—
A goodly gift indeed, from blossom-babies
　　To human-kind.

THE SONG OF
THE SWEET PEA FAIRIES

Here Sweet Peas are climbing;
   Here's the Sweet Pea rhyme!
Here are the little tendrils,
   Helping them to climb.

Here are the sweetest colours;
   Fragrance very sweet;
Here are the silky pods of peas,
   Not for us to eat!

Here's a fairy sister,
   Trying on with care
Such a grand new bonnet
   For the baby there.

Does it suit you, Baby?
   Yes, I really think
Nothing's more becoming
   Than this pretty pink!

DEVELOPMENT

I first focused my eyes on . . . .

. . . .

Smiled . . . .

Slept through the night . . . .

Laughed . . . .

Rolled over . . . .

Sat up . . . .

DEVELOPMENT

Moved from my cradle to my bed . .

. . . .

I ate my first real food on . . . .

. . . .

It was . . . .

I drank from a cup by myself on . . .

. . . .

Had my hair cut . . . .

(stick down
lock of hair)

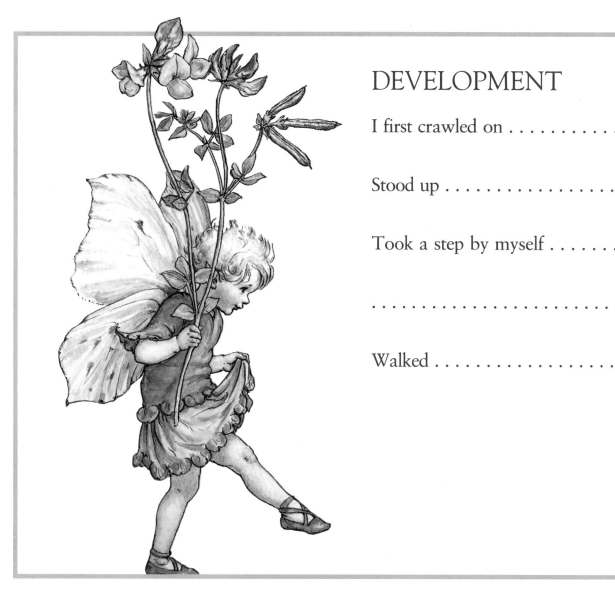

DEVELOPMENT

I first crawled on . . . .

Stood up . . . .

Took a step by myself . . . .

. . . .

Walked . . . .

DEVELOPMENT

My First Words

. . . .

. . . .

(photo)

. . . .

. . . .

Aged . . . . .

THINGS I LIKE

The toys I like best are . . . .

. . . .

Nursery rhymes . . . .

. . . .

Food . . . .

Animals . . . .

Games . . . .

. . . .

(photo)

Aged . . . .

Things I don't like . . . .

. . . .

OUTINGS

Place . . . .

. . . . Date . . . .

Place . . . .

. . . . Date . . . .

Place . . . .

. . . . Date . . . .

Place . . . .

. . . . Date . . . .

MY FIRST TRAVELS

Dates . . . .

Place . . . .

Activities . . . .

. . . .

. . . .

. . . .

. . . .

. . . .

(photo)

Aged . . . .

MY FIRST CHRISTMAS

Place . . . .

The weather was . . . .

. . . .

Other people there were . . . .

. . . .

. . . .

. . . .

. . . .

My presents were

. . . .

From . . . .

(photo)

. . . .

From . . . .

. . . .

From . . . .

Aged . . . .

MY FIRST BIRTHDAY

Date. . . . .

Place. . . . .

The weather was . . . .

Other people there were . . . .

. . . .

. . . .

Games we played were . . . .

. . . .

My presents were

. . . .

From . . . .

(photo)

. . . .

From . . . .

. . . .

From . . . .

Aged . . . .

PHOTOGRAPHS

FREDERICK WARNE

Published by the Penguin Group
27 Wrights Lane, London W8 5TZ, England
Penguin Books USA Inc., 375 Hudson Street, New York, New York 10014, USA
Penguin Books Australia Ltd, Ringwood, Victoria, Australia
Penguin Books Canada Ltd, 10 Alcorn Avenue, Toronto, Ontario, Canada M4V 3B2
Penguin Books (NZ) Ltd, 182-190 Wairau Road, Auckland 10, New Zealand

Penguin Books Ltd, Registered Offices: Harmondsworth, Middlesex, England

First published 1991
7 9 10 8 6

ISBN 0 7232 3787 5

Colour origination by Anglia Graphics Ltd.
Printed and·bound in Great Britain by
William Clowes Limited, Beccles and London